The Road to Donaguile

Douglas.

" Zo n-éirigíd an bóżan leat

Herbert O'Driscoll.

The Road to Donaguile

A Celtic Spiritual Journey

৩৫

Herbert O'Driscoll

COWLEY PUBLICATIONS
Cambridge · Boston
Massachusetts

Published in the United States of America by Cowley
Publications, a division of the Society of St. John the
Evangelist. No portion of this book may be reproduced, stored
in or introduced into a retrieval system, or transmitted, in any
form or by any means—including photocopying—without the
prior written permission of Cowley Publications, except in the
case of brief quotations embodied in critical articles and
reviews.

Library of Congress Cataloging-in-Publication Data:
O'Driscoll, Herbert.
   The road to Donaguile : a Celtic spiritual journey /
   Herbert O'Driscoll.
         p.   cm.
   ISBN 1-56101-173-8 (alk. paper)
   1. O'Driscoll, Herbert—Childhood and youth. 2. Church of
   Ireland—Clergy—Biography. 3. Anglican Communion—
   Clergy—Biography. 4. Celts—Religion. 5. Spiritual life.
   I. Title.
BX5595.O36 A3 2000
283'.092—dc21   99-049301
[B]
Portions of this book previously appeared in *A Doorway in Time.*
Cynthia Shattuck, editor; Vicki Black, copyeditor and designer
This book was printed in Canada on recycled, acid-free paper.

Cowley Publications
28 Temple Place Boston, Massachusetts 02111
800-225-1534   www.cowley.org

For my parents, brothers, and cousins,
companions on the road to Donaguile

ᄋᄋ

Contents

࿓

Acknowledgments

Fifteen years ago, encouraged by my then editor and now friend, Avery Brooke, I wrote a book called *A Doorway in Time,* memories of growing up as a Church of Ireland child in the newly born Irish Republic. Recently, invited and encouraged by Cynthia Shattuck at Cowley, I have been given an opportunity to revisit those times and places, recalling much that had not previously emerged from memory.

I am deeply grateful for my editor's help in shaping this remembering. I hope that anyone who read *A Doorway in Time* will wish to discover what else lies beyond that doorway, and that those who take *The Road to Donaguile* for the first time will find themselves recalling with pleasure remembered experiences of their own growing years.

one

Remembering Donaguile

I said goodbye to Donaguile almost casually. We were driving south from Dublin to Kilkenny and towards mid-morning we came down past the parish church where my grandparents are buried, crossed the stone bridge over the river, and drove slowly up through the town square.

There came a moment when we could either turn left for Kilkenny—twelve miles away—or go straight ahead up the hill about a mile and a half to the gates of Donaguile. I turned left, almost as if someone other than myself had made the decision. In doing so I realized that the spell of childhood had been broken and I could from now on, if I wished, return to the farm and the little roads of Donaguile as an adult. Hitherto, even though I was in my middle sixties and had visited once every few years, I had always returned here as a if child: I would find myself anticipating the sights—the apple orchard—and the sounds—the lazy cackle of a hen—that I had seen and heard in childhood summers here.

In recent decades we have become familiar with many books on the human life cycle. It is hard to read them without getting the illusion that the various stages of life end and begin rather neatly, as if we cross a threshold from one room of time to another. The truth is that our transitions are gradual and largely unconscious. But what is also true is that a certain moment of consciousness, an outwardly simple event or action or word, can make us realize that a transition has already taken place, not in this moment of awareness but at some previous time we have only just come to recognize.

For me the simple act of turning left in the town square in Castlecomer rather than driving up the hill familiar since childhood showed me suddenly and vividly that I had passed to another stage of my life This was made even more startling for me because all the way down from Dublin I had intended to drive to the farmhouse, even if only to stop at the end of the yard, look through the gates, then turn the car and drive away. This had been the pattern of my visits in recent years.

In the moments of turning down Kilkenny street and heading out of the small town of Castlecomer, I realized again how we can retain elements of childhood long after its actual years have passed. The cord of time, long loosened in many ways, still chooses certain things to link us to early years. For me, that certain thing has been Donaguile: my grandfather's farm, my mother's childhood home, and the place where we spent summer vacations in the years before boarding school brought an end to the annual journeys.

For years there were three of us—my mother, my younger brother, and I—making the annual pilgrimage from the small city of Cork where we lived. Then, when I was nine, our youngest brother was born and duly joined the expedition. Father would come later when he was free from the office for a couple of weeks. We three boys were quite widely spaced in age. I was the eldest, the others four and almost ten years younger. As the years of childhood went on, the family of cousins on the farm grew—seven in all—so there were always playmates of the right age for my brothers. I, who had experienced the farm for four or five years as a solitary child, continued to move largely in my own world. To this day, when we talk about the farm, I will mention some event I remember only to receive blank stares from my brothers, even about events that are so vivid to me I am quite sure they could never have forgotten them.

However, one event that all three of us do remember vividly is the day in the hay barn. That year we must have stayed later on the farm than usual. It must have been late August. All the hay was in, dragged in from the field with the horses and forked up higher and higher in the barn by the hard work of our two uncles, our grandfather, and John the hired man. I emphasize the labor involved to explain the reason for what happened.

There is something wonderful to a child about the idea of putting a ladder to the open side of a barn, climbing up, and then lying on the warm dry hay. For three boys aged fourteen, ten, and four, it is even more wonderful to start jumping on the hay. Soon we are throwing it at one another, hay going every which way. Suddenly there is a bellow of rage and our grandfather is shaking his fist at us. We know there is no time to use the ladder. The back of the barn is next to a raised bank. We slide down the side of the hay, jump from the bank, and run. Our destination is the house recently purchased by one of our uncles. We know our mother is down there. We also know we are in trouble when we see our other uncle bursting from the farmhouse and coming after us. We have a good head start, at least the two of us who are older have. The youngest is terrified and calling us to wait for him, but survival wins over solidarity and he is left far behind. We come to what was known in Ireland as a five bar gate. I climb over the top, my brother goes through the middle gap in the bars, and the youngest of us—already passed by and now far behind our uncle—crawls under the gate, whimpering in fear, his eyes like saucers.

I have a vague memory of reaching the other house and finding our mother, behind whom—I bow my head in shame—we trembled, waiting for our uncle to arrive, our youngest brother in tow, now no longer terrified that his uncle is going to tear him limb from limb! All I recall is that mother managed to save us from punishment.

Another memory we all share is that painful day when two of us decided to ride the patient and long-suffering farm donkey. We find some old sacking to make do as a saddle. One of us holds the unwilling and rather startled donkey while the other mounts. Now the second would-be rider lets the donkey's head go and scrambles onto his back as he already begins to move away. Quickly the donkey gathers momentum. We have nothing to hang on to other than the slightly longer hairs of the donkey's neck. My brother has only me to hang on to.

We are shouting in mingled excitement and alarm. Suddenly we realize that we cannot guide the progress of the donkey and he is heading for a huge bed of tall nettles. Helplessly we see the nettles getting nearer and nearer. By now we are gradually sliding sideways on the donkey's back. We know with a horrible certainty what is about to happen—and it does! We are deposited among the nettles. They sting our hands, legs, and faces as we shout and wail. The donkey shakes his head, flaps his great ears, kicks up his heels as if to say good riddance to us, and disappears. We head for home, mother, and comfort.

Let me tell you a little more about Donaguile. I have never been quite sure whether it is merely the name of my grandfather's farm—now no longer in the family—or the name of the surrounding townland. The term townland will sound strange so I need to give it some context. Old societies tend to have many layers of naming. In Ireland there have been provinces, such as Leinster and Munster, for at least two millennia. Within the provinces today there are counties, such as Wicklow, Roscommon, Kerry. These names are much later, at least in their present anglicized forms. The Normans brought organization to what they saw as Celtic disorganization. Soon, with the counties—small enough already—there came the names of townlands. Today we would consider them districts.

In the small world of a child these townlands were distant places. We had relatives in a townland called Cloneen. We visited one summer, harnessing the horse and trap, throwing in rugs and cushions for the long journey, especially the nighttime return. The journey took a couple of hours each way. Other townlands had names such as

Ballyraggett, Boharnafay, Clasduff, and Sliguff. Furthermore, many farms would themselves be named, and within these farms even the fields would have a name.

Only a few months ago I sat beside my mother's hospital bed in the last days of her life as she moved in and out of consciousness following a massive stroke. It was near midnight and I was waiting for my brother to spell me. I leaned forward towards my mother's unseeing eyes and said, "Mother, I can remember that the Barn Field was next to the house in Donaguile. What was the name of the next field?"

At first there was only silence, the low hiss of the oxygen easing her breathing. Then she began to name the fields, working her way up the long gentle slope of the valley beyond the house. I realized again that the names of the fields when said in succession become—as does so much Irish utterance— a kind of poetry, a singing rather than a mere listing. The Hill Field, the Barn Field, Back of Martin's, Darby's Haggart, Back of Brennan's, the Hayseed, the Horse Field, Over Darby's.

As I listened I became a child again, as I suspect my mother was, freeing herself from her weakened body and damaged brain, both of us walking together up through the fields, pausing to open each gate and carefully close it again, until we came to the last field before the borders of the neighboring farm. From here we could turn and look down across the fields, down to where the smoke rose lazily from the farmhouse chimney. We could watch my grandfather herding the cows into the barn for milking, the barking of Billy the farm dog floating up to us on the quiet evening air.

☙☙
two

The Geography
of Childhood

I am standing at the top of the courtyard onto which the front doors of about a dozen small houses open. On one of the doors the black crepe hangs on the chipped paint. I am ten years old. An elderly neighbor, Mrs. Griffin, is dying.

The Angelus bell is still ringing over the small city of Cork where we live. I am standing, holding a ball. Suddenly around the small corner shop at the end of the courtyard a large, florid, black-cassocked priest appears. As if by prearranged signal, like an opera chorus appearing from the wings of a stage as the main actor takes center place, doors open and neighbors appear. All play stops among us children. Addressing the street in general, the priest shouts, "Is she dead yet?"

The question ricochets along the courtyard of houses, seeming to a child to assume a quality greater and more solemn than human inquiry. It is as if God is requiring a report on the condition of a soul. All the neighbors shake their heads. The black clad figure turns and goes up and over the hill beyond which the bell tower booming the Angelus stands against the evening sun.

For me it was a many layered moment. Only in adulthood will its meaning begin to unfold. Certainly there was the realization that Mrs. Griffin was part of a communal world, her dying somehow our shared care and terror, as her living had been part of a network of friendships and daily familiarities. About the church a mingled message was received. On the one hand it seemed to stand vast and unpitying, devoid of gentleness and any outward love. On the other hand, at least to a child, a great truth was communicated on that summer evening, the perception of a powerful matter-of-factness in the face of death. At some level I became aware that there existed a power that refused to be impressed by the dread unseen visitor that inhabited the Griffin's house behind the crepe-covered door and the closed lace curtains and the yellow blinds. I began to perceive, however dimly, that while that ancient enemy would be allowed his time on our street, there was no longer cause for concern. Mrs. Griffin, as we all knew, had already been prepared for death by confession and shriving. She had been anointed with the oil of extreme unction. Death could be allowed the paltry booty of her body. Ancient and implacable boundaries of word and sacrament had been placed about death's domain and arrogant claims.

The Angelus bell falls silent. Front doors close again. The ball is thrown back into play. Mrs. Griffin's soul is safe among a community of children playing, as childhood does, on the boundary line of time and eternity. Later there would come the Requiem Mass, surrounding her with a community possessing mysteries older and wiser and lovelier than the illusions we call time past, time present, time future. We tend to think that faith comes on the carefully constructed highways of teaching, study, and information. Yet who knows by what unexpected byways of childhood experience there comes a much deeper perception of what lies at the heart of things?

To grow up in the south of Ireland in the 1930s was to inhabit a sacred universe. It was, I now realize, to live in the last lingering twilight of a medieval, and to some extent, feudal world. It was not an ideal universe nor even a particularly moral one, as time and events have frequently shown. It was, however, a sacred world. Behind or hidden in the visibilities and tangibilities of the everyday, another level of reality was always assumed. The seen was surrounded by the unseen, which, to some people and at some unexpected moments, afforded glimpses of either its beauty or its terror, its gift or its threat.

In that world there was always the web of family, nuclear and extended, long before these neat impersonal labels became attached to life and relationships. The houses of uncles and aunts stood within walking distance in the small city of Cork, founded as it was in Norse times on the marshes surrounding the River Lee on the south coast. These homes were the scenes of mingled and transitory intimacies and antagonisms but always they were unquestionably family.

There were Sunday visits to the large red-bricked institution known as The Home for Protestant Incurables, where we would visit my paternal grandmother. As I recall that name—the HPI, as my parents would refer to it—I realize how unyielding was the language of that older society: honest, unpretending, to us today unpitying. Outside the city on a green hillside stood the Lunatic Asylum. Elsewhere there was a building gently curtained, its entrance surrounded by flowers but with the words "The Rest for the Dying" cut into the stone archway above the door.

My grandmother awaited the regular visits of my father and his brothers. I usually accompanied my father. My grandmother had high cheekbones and flared eyebrows and her long white hair cascaded over heaped high pillows. Her blue-veined skin rippled and shone parchment-smooth as she placed fresh minted golden pennies in each pocket of my new suit, her hands touching my body like whispering ghosts on the edge of being corporeal. To this day I have never traced the custom she called "hanselling," which she spoke of vaguely as a protection. I suspect it was a custom born out of ancient fears felt in the forests and the high places

15

whose last remnants still ringed the city after centuries of decimation.

If the surrounding hills held the city in their embrace and set limits to our horizons—and remember how much more possible this was in a society without automobiles—it was the river that allowed us glimpses of a greater world. As a small boy I would be taken for a daily walk along the river. I was getting just old enough to look over the low wall into the dark depths of its flow. Every few hundred yards there would be a break in the wall where steps would go down until they became green with moss and weed and disappeared into the water under the bows of the moored rowing boats left there by fishermen. Further away, where the river broadened into a wide lake and then turned south for the distant harbor, stood Blackrock Castle. Romantically battlemented, the narrow slits in its walls hid infinite dark possibilities to a child's mind. Sometimes, as I got older and could walk further, my mother would go as far as the turn in the river and I would look down to what seemed distant villages on the way to the harbor itself.

One wonderful day my father tells me that he will have a rare free Saturday soon and perhaps we could get the train and go to Cobh (pronounced Cove) and see the harbor. The journey is about twelve miles. How pathetic such a distance sounds today; how magical beyond words it was then. I had been in the railway station but never to catch a train. I had watched as trains left the station, wondering about the distant places they were bound for. Today is different. Today we go to the small window to buy our return tickets for what my father still calls Queenstown. Only recently has the name been changed, now that the new Irish Republic has come into being. He has regaled me with tales about the harbor, how it is so large that it can contain the whole British fleet. He tells me of the day when he was taken to Queenstown by his father the week that Queen Victoria died, when every ship in the harbor was at half-mast and festooned with black bunting. Along the river the train travels, first easterly in direction until we get to Queenstown, or Cobh Junction, then turning south with the course of the river.

Much of the day has been forgotten, save for some moments that remain like old prints in the mind. My father is pointing to the mouth of the harbor, far in the distance. He shows me the two great forts that guard the entrance. He tells me that just beyond that point is the open ocean, the Atlantic, and only a few miles beyond the forts lies the wreck of the *Lusitania,* sunk by the Germans with great loss of life. Such information is never received by a small boy merely as information. The wonder and mystery of such an event reverberates in a child's mind. I am out there beyond the forts, beyond the guns, beyond the calm waters of the harbor, out in the heaving ocean. The outline of the wreck looms in the dark depths.

Later in the day, when we have shared the lunch made for us by my mother, we are sitting on a park bench looking out across the water towards the south. Suddenly my father jumps up and cries, "Look! Out there! As far as you can see!" He points my eyes to the south, far out beyond the mouth of the harbor and the last of the land, out to where a small grey shape is moving westward over the ocean. "It's the Hindenburg," my father cries, "the big new German airship! It's sailing to America." We stand together transfixed with excitement and wonder. For a moment we are in touch with the great world glimpsed in the front page of the evening newspaper and the voices of the crackling radio in the corner of the kitchen. The moment eclipses everything else in the day and makes my father a purveyor of wonder and high achievement in my eyes. It is as if he has personally arranged for this wonderful conjunction of time when the great ship and our train journey intersect and the world comes to our doorstep.

I recall nothing else. I suspect I slept for the train journey home. It had been a most memorable day, all the more so because of having my father's company. I realize now that the day enlarged my little world. I had seen the harbor, until then almost mythical in my imagination. I had almost glimpsed the ocean that lay beyond. I had even seen a great airship bound for America. The very fact of seeing that grey shape flying west across the late afternoon sky allowed me to imagine the unimaginable—traveling to America!

There were, of course, other moments with my father. I am intrigued to realize now that the most easily remembered are those moments when he pointed me outside my immediate world. Three times a week the big white and blue car and passenger ferry would come from Fishguard in Wales, and we would go down to look at it, sometimes docking, sometimes leaving. I would hear of the train that would be waiting for it in Fishguard to whirl its passengers to London. At other times I would be shown my father's latest foray into amateur radio. We would sit down and listen to the strange sounds of the world of shortwave radio, hearing voices that would come into the room for a moment from some infinitely distant place and then fade again.

I wonder now whether my father was unconsciously expressing a longing to escape from the prison that his job had become. He was responsible for distributing the products of the largest bakery in the country during the war years, when almost every means of distribution was functioning with the greatest difficulty. I realize now that my father lived with unrelenting stress and frustration, both of which destroyed his health and robbed him of energy to participate in our lives. Because he loved us and our mother deeply, this only added to his sense of defeat and futility. I suspect that his great fear was that his children would also become prisoners of a society which at that time held little opportunity for its new generation.

Now it is October of 1939 and war has been declared. I am nearly eleven and my birthday is approaching. In one of the stores downtown I have seen a toy gun that fires pellets. Others in school have them. To say that I want one is an understatement. The toy gun occupies my waking and sleeping thoughts. It costs six shillings—such a small amount, yet war has brought something else to our house, a slashing attack on my father's already modest salary. The whole office staff salary scale has been reduced by one-third without notice. No union exists for his world of white collar workers. He is helpless. My brother and I hear him sobbing one day with our mother and we are frightened. Yet, in the fashion of childhood, this knowledge does not still my longing for the gun.

My birthday nears. My mother warns me that it may not be possible to buy the toy gun. The day before my birthday comes. I return from school in the mid-afternoon on a bright day lit by the weak sunshine of early winter in Ireland. There is no one at home when I turn the key in the door and go into the kitchen. A bright ray of sun is playing on the kitchen table, and in that sunlight shine three silver florins—six shillings. Beside them is a note from my father wishing me a happy birthday and telling me to go downtown and get the toy gun.

I am just old enough to feel two things simultaneously: the unmitigated joy of a child at getting what I want more than anything else in the world, and the beginning of the realization of how much my father loves me and at what cost.

୧୧
three

All Our
Yesterdays

I remember a particular Saturday afternoon when the Wolf Cubs had gathered at a suburban bus stop near the church. The weather had cleared, so it was decided we could have our promised outing. We clambered and pushed our way up the narrow steps of the double decker, running towards the front seats, there to argue and laugh and shout until the last of the city had passed and the green fields stretched ahead, and the bus came to the end of its run.

I realize now that on that Saturday afternoon in 1936 the city was still the creature of the countryside. The rolling green ocean of fields allowed the existence of the city as an island set within its eternal flow. To come out of the city, as we were doing that day, was to return to a home only recently left. In fact, to live in that long ago city of Cork, a gathering of about seventy-five thousand souls, was hardly to leave the countryside at all. Every morning, a mile or two from our house, while the city still slept, Mr. Barry milked his cows, put the milk in a large churn with a silver tap, harnessed his horse to the well-sprung buggy, trotted into the city, and delivered his milk door to door. He would measure it from a gleaming metal pint container with a long curved bronze handle. The milk would flow into multicolored and variously shaped jugs held for him by housewives, among them my mother. Faithful to ancient custom, Mr Barry always added what he called a "tilly." The expression comes from the old Gaelic word *tuilleadh* that means something extra, what the Bible means when it speaks of "good measure, pressed down, running over."

We pour out of the bus and are formed into a ragged line by our cub master. It is almost impossible to keep us in line because we are excited. We are about to carry out a favorite Saturday game: we are going to play in the old fort on the nearby hillside. We do not refer to it as a fort. Although we are not yet aware of it, Latin has always had an uneasy truce on this island with a tongue as old, if not older. Instead, we call the circular earthworks that surround the hilltop "the rath," a word that has come to us with the dreaded marauders from the north sea, the Vikings.

Half of us will defend the rath, half will scatter and then attack. The defenders begin their climb up the hill to take their positions within the circle. With them they take the flag that will be planted in the middle of the rath and that we will do our best to capture.

This Saturday I am picked to be an attacker. The cub master repeats his instructions and we scatter in the neighboring fields and hedges and ditches. Each of us is now alone in the still afternoon. I look up the sloping hillside to where the small white clouds move across the sky from the southwest, bringing with them warm breezes from the gulf stream. At first the world is silent, then I am aware of my own heartbeat, quickened by excitement. I hear a rhythmic sound nearby: a cow is chewing the cud, her calm brown eyes gazing in detached curiosity at this small human visitor lying in the grass nearby. Far away the sound of a car engine is carried on the air.

I am no longer merely a Wolf Cub. It is no longer 1936. I am a Norseman and it is the tenth century. We have just come up the river in our longboats, moored them, and have headed inland for this brief foray. It has to be completed swiftly because we have to return to the safety of the ships before nightfall.

I turn over on my stomach and look through the long heavy grass at the distant rath. I am quite certain that I am invisible to the defenders. Thus the next hour is spent, carefully making my approach, lying still for long periods, now and then hearing shouts as another attacker rushes the defenses and is caught. I use the bushes, the hedges, the trees—crouching, sliding, creeping, running. I signal at last to another attacker to make a diversion. As he does, three of us rush towards the earthworks. We bottle up our shouts until we have climbed to the top and are charging down the inner slope, rushing towards the flag pole that sticks out of the grass at an angle. To touch it we have to run the gauntlet of the defenders. Once tackled by a defender we are considered dead, out of the game. We know that we play where once life and death were anything but a game. The grass we ran on and lay upon was rich in blood long since dried and drained into the earth.

I realize now that in that Ireland of the years before the Second World War the past was primary. It was as if a whole people had willed themselves into occupying the past as ultimate reality. To come to Dublin from the provinces was to stand in the high vault of the general post office and read the haunting lyrical idealism of the leaders of the 1916 rebellion. To cycle in the Dublin and Wicklow Mountains was to look for the tortuous journey taken by the two young fugitives, Hugh O'Neill and Hugh O'Donnell, as they made their escape from Dublin Castle in the frigid winter of 1591. O'Donnell became the last of the old Gaelic kings and the bitter enemy of Elizabeth I in then far away London.

To arrive in Clifden in west Connemara, to cycle out to the narrow rough road to the headland, the wind lifting the Atlantic into white horses riding the dark waves, was instinctively to recall the desperate efforts of the scattered remains of the Spanish Armada to make any harbor on this formidable and foreign coast. To drive southeast towards Dublin, the fields of Meath darkening in the evening, was to look towards the distant mounds that had once been Tara and the place of the high kings of Ireland in the centuries before the new religion of the cross came. To round the Old Head of Kinsale, the small inboard engine laboring and racing as the fishing boat bucked and reared in the tumble of coastal currents, was to sail among the remembered masts of the great French fleet that waited there in vain in 1601, hoping to rendezvous with an Irish army from the north, both of them fated to suffer a defeat that spelled the end of sustained and organized Gaelic military power.

To see the woods on the ridges of the hills, dark green against the sky, sharply delineated by centuries of deforestation, was to think of the legendary warriors of the Fianna and the baying of their wolf hounds as they crashed through the forests in pursuit of deer long gone from now stone-walled domesticated pastures. To see those same stone walls, their worn tumbled lines outlining narrow roads and tiny holdings, the grassy plots between them scabrous and pockmarked with scattered stones, was to recall the work projects of the terrible famine years of the 1840s, memorials to the desperate efforts of more compassionate landlords to breathe life into an economy already dead.

Thus did the present fade into unreality before the vivid images and tragedies of the past. By its determination to use the past to give motivation and political energy to the fledgling new republic, the government was helping to create a generation for whom, by a terrible irony, the past would become the present and memory become what we know today as virtual reality.

I mention this love affair with time in the Irish psyche because of the ambiguous gifts it brings. To me personally it brought a sense of stability in the possession of a long story, but there are those for whom this ability to accord to all layers of time equal reality gives something else. It seems to provide a kind of embalming fluid for hatred and prejudice. It can kindle an endless twilight where no battle is ever ended, no issue ever settled, no revenge satisfied, where church bells forever toll of a thousand wrongs and no bell rings in the new.

We end our Wolf Cub Saturday with stained clothes, earth on our knees, hands sticky from jam sandwiches. We come down the hilly fields to the country lane that leads eventually to the main road and the bus stop. Here, where the roads join, there is a shrine. These shrines were totally taken for granted in childhood, the eyeless face of the plaster-cast figure looking back to the martyrdom of some minor saint. The military skirmish this shrine also memorializes took place some years before I was born, yet it would, and still does, remain as the echo chamber for the shouts of men long dead and the rattle of gunfire long silenced.

We scramble onto the bus, once again fighting to be first up to the upper deck and first into a front seat. We argue in loud voices about which side won our Saturday battle. By the time we arrive back in the city the voices have died down as tiredness sets in. Our parents are waiting for us at the church hall. Even Vikings get weary and have to turn for home and bed.

Corpus Christi

In adult life I have seldom experienced the total silencing and immobilizing of a city. I remember this fact occurring to me as I watched the funeral of President John F. Kennedy on television, looking at the streets lined with mourners, the total absence of traffic, the silence in which the drums beat steadily. But even then I could not experience the full effect of that stillness because I was not there. I was a spectator, looking through the tiny window of television, experiencing a certain sense of awe, yet finally being outside.

As a child I do remember a city becoming silent and still, an experience that was all the more awe inspiring because I stood in its streets as a small boy. It was 1937. I was nine years old and I said yes to my friend Jim's invitation to go downtown to watch the procession. I was not quite sure what the procession was, but it sounded good so we set off.

In those days downtown was not very far away. As we went we joined a steadily growing stream of adults and children heading in the same direction. In the distance we could hear church bells ringing. We crossed Saint Patrick's Bridge into the wide curved boulevard that was the heart of the city. Its new appearance and clean exteriors came from the fact that one whole side of the street had been burnt in the "troubles" less than twenty years before, necessitating its complete rebuilding. That is where the crowds were assembling.

My memory is that it was a happy, boisterous crowd. This in itself was a revelation to me. Even though we were about to be part of what I understood to be a religious occasion—the precise nature of which I only vaguely understood—we could hear cheerful salutations being exchanged across the crowd, joking remarks here and there, lots of laughter. In the upper windows of the large stores people waved to others whom they knew in the crowd. Presumably they were staff members taking advantage of their place of work to get a good view.

I was puzzled because my own Church of Ireland (Anglican) services were always quiet and solemn affairs.

As we waited the black and white van of Saint John's Ambulance passed along through the crowd, sobering everyone for a moment because it could only mean that someone already needed medical attention. A little later the whole crowd roared encouragement as a couple of young men began to climb the statue of Father Matthew to get a better view. A priest who in his lifetime had done much good work in the city, he now stood in dark immobility on a high block of stone, presiding benignly over the city growing around him. On this and other occasions the good Father provided a wonderful perch for anyone daring enough to see as far as he or she wished.

At what seemed a great distance I could hear the sound of a band. It turned out to be an army band and its music was slow and solemn, probably to emphasize that the event was a serious one in spite of any levity among us spectators. People strained to look back in the direction of the bridge. We children were given free rein to push and work our way through the crowd towards the front row, where we found policemen patrolling the edges of the crowd. There Jim and I could see everything there was to see.

My memory of the order of things is now vague, but I recall the band came first, the sun glinting on brass instruments, the leader resplendent in white gloves and carrying a staff with which he beat time for those behind him. Being an army band, its passing filled the crowd with pride: up to that time British army bands were the only army bands seen and heard by the older generation. Here was a band of the Irish army, resplendent in their green uniforms, and behind them came a body of soldiers, complete with rifles.

There were other bands, though whether they came from communities outside the city or not I simply do not know. At one stage there was a pipe band, this time with saffron kilts swinging and a pipe major who hurled his staff in the air. Every time it seemed to go higher and higher and to turn more times, and every time we watched for him to let it drop and he never did!

Then came the children. Whenever I read of the Children's Crusade in the Middle Ages I think of this day and this occasion. The schools of the city were closed—even our school because it was a public holiday—so the church commandeered their pupils for the procession. The ruddy Irish faces of the Wolf Cubs, Boy Scouts, and Girl Guides were beaming with excitement and self-importance at being part of the occasion, dressed in their uniforms. No effort was made to get them to walk in step. They flowed along in a solid mass, looking around for parents and grandparents, waving in every direction. From all sides there would be greeting from the crowd. "There's Bridey," a voice would shout. "Sure isn't she lovely!" Or, "There's Sean. Good man, Sean!" Sean and Bridey would grin shyly and wave again before being swept on in the flow.

Then there came the many Catholic organizations: the Legion of Mary, the Confraternity of the Blessed Sacrament, the Solidarity of Blessed Oliver Plunkett, and, most impressive of all, the Knights of Columbus. As soon as they appeared silence fell once again as their black robes and drawn swords passed us by. For many of us small boys the drawn swords made the day.

But the silence deepened when the next part of the procession rounded the curve of the street. Here

was the heart of the occasion, the reason for everything—the bands, the uniforms, the crowds, the
empty city streets around the center of the city, the
closed offices and shops. The first thing I saw was
the white and gold canopy waving up and down as
it was carried by priests. As it came nearer I saw
that it was preceded and followed by other clergy in
their robes, among them a figure who I now realize
was the bishop. He was attended by priests and
blessed us all as he walked, looking this way and
that in the crowd. The thought occurred to me that
he might in some mysterious way know that there
was a Protestant child on the edge of the crowd and
disapprove. He looked like someone who would
have mysterious ways of knowing everything, and
so I was relieved when he passed by leaving us
undetected.

The white and gold canopy sheltered a round
disc of gold on a long pole that was carried by a tall
robed figure. In the center of the gold was a small
pale circle. I did not know what it was, and neither
did Jim. Instinctively we did not ask anyone around
us, chiefly because we could see that this was a most
solemn moment for everyone. The following
Sunday we asked Miss Greenish, our white-haired

and gentle Sunday school teacher whom I remember to this day very vividly. She gave us a wise, simple, short answer. She said that what we had seen was the Sacred Host or the Bread of the Mass, which was in a very mysterious way the Body of Our Lord. That is why everyone knelt down as it passed, and that was why the day had been given its name—Corpus Christi, which means the Body of Christ. I remember that I found it a perfectly reasonable and satisfying reply. I realize now that we were fortunate in asking Miss Greenish, who had the wisdom and the sensitivity—not to mention the breadth of mind—not to give us an answer in the sectarian terms we would have heard from many others, who would have dismissed everything about the great day as Roman superstition.

For me the moment of the passing of the canopied monstrance stayed for the rest of my life. For all I know it may well have been one of those unrealized moments of childhood that led to priesthood and ministry. The thing I remember most clearly was that, at the moment when we realized that we should genuflect with everybody else, Jim suddenly said "Jesus!" in a loud, hoarse whisper, and down he went, pulling me with him.

The power of the moment was in the way the silence of the crowd changed to a strange sound, a kind of whispering wave moving through them as they all—Jim and I among them—knelt for the passing of the Host. Around us everyone made the quick, almost furtive, sign of the cross that was for so long utterly natural in Irish life; it was made quickly because it was made so often throughout any normal working day. As we stayed down on one knee Jim and I had a certain weight of guilt as to what our parents would say if some well-meaning neighbor reported our newly acquired Catholic devotion!

My memories fade after that moment. I remember that there were some policemen, some nurses. Probably there were men and women representing civic associations and professions. As I think back on that wonderful day, it seems that the gift given to me by the experience was a glimpse of a world made whole. I witnessed a society, a city, a country—because there would have been processions in other cities too—captured by the demand of the sacred and giving it absolute precedence over everything else, over commerce, schooling, sports, institutional life of every kind. I think I was in some sense given a glimpse of what was once called Christendom just before it was to disappear. I shall probably never see anything like it again in my lifetime, but for that very reason I treasure the memory all the more.

The memory also serves as a future hope for the fragmented culture I now live in. I would not for a moment expect elements of social and cultural wholeness to return in the same way. The canopy, the golden circle, the bishop, the swords of the Knights and the guns of the soldiers have passed and will not come again in the same way. But the memory of the social unity of the day makes me look for signs of wholeness about me, however faint and tenuous.

I think too that I was touched by what I could not then name, and even now can only grope to call mystery and transcendence. A world passed by that I was privileged to see because of a childish indiscretion—or was the indiscretion of Jim's invitation something far more? The church that I watched passing by was at that time glorious and confident, even imperial in its capacity to discipline and rule and punish. But in spite of whatever faults are now ascribed to it in a very different age, it challenged the so-called real world to halt its restless activities and to acknowledge and dare to believe in a world even more real. Such were the gifts of Corpus Christi to a wide-eyed Protestant child caught up in the surge of a vast, never-to-be-forgotten Catholic tide.

ᎪᎪ
five

The Road to
Donaguile

D istant from the small city where we lived but
still intensely real was our mother's home, a
place of grandparents, uncles, aunts, and ever mul-
tiplying cousins, the farm flowing up the side of a
valley where it was always summer. At some level
of perception I am aware of other seasons, but they
existed only in conversations overheard. In a
dreamlike way—before my brother was born and I
was still little more than a toddler—I remember
once seeing the fields white with a light covering of
snow, the calves coming to their buckets of feed
held by my grandfather's hand, their tiny horned

heads banging against the metal in their eagerness to feed.

For the most part, seasons other than summer came and went in another time and universe where adults lived a sterner and separate life. For me, days ended on the farm when the evening brought out the oil lamps or when the trees at the end of the driveway hidden by the darkness lashed and hissed in a night wind. In the morning there was water to be carried from the depths of the moss-lined cavern where the well lay. During the days there was hay to be brought in from distant fields, drawn by the swelling haunches of great horses on whose foreheads flies stood dark and thick. Infinitely distant, seen only from the fields above the house, a blue mountain named Mount Leinster beckoned at the frontier of my childhood world.

Here in these fields was the other part of my life, where the city was forgotten and I roamed at will. Many years were to go by before I inadvertently learned how deeply connected I had become to these fields and this part of my family. It was a summer in the mid-1960s when my wife and I took our children to visit Ireland. We were near the end of our stay. We had taken them hither and yon, pointing to this and that from our own lives, often I suspect to the mystification of the children, aged about ten, eight, and five. We had visited Dublin, gone down to Cork, met an elderly uncle and aunt of mine as well as cousins, and made an utterly ridiculous attempt to do the Ring of Kerry in a single day, complete with children! The Ring named the magnificent drive—but on twisting, narrow roads—that took us over the last mountain range of west Cork, continuing west around the wild Atlantic coast before turning inland for Killarney and, for us that day, the long darkening drive back to Cork city.

We survived, of course, as families usually do, but the incident that stands out for me is the ending of our visit to my now adult cousins who were once the children of the farm at Donaguile. By then they too had children of their own. We had had a good few hours together, reminiscing, asking after this person and that, sharing a meal. The time came to leave. We had said other goodbyes in the weeks of this holiday. Though both of us parents had grown up in Ireland, we had by this time no longings to return. Encounters and partings had been pleasant and easy, but this time things changed without any warning. We climbed into the station wagon and were moving away, everyone waving, the children calling out, when suddenly I found myself crying uncontrollably. The children were quite puzzled, even a little concerned at this parental weeping, and greatly relieved when it was over. For me had come the realization of how large a part the world of the farm had played in my life.

Every July for the first fifteen years of my life we would prepare to go to the farm. We would stay there about a month, sometimes more, and my father would come for his annual two-weeks holiday. In a way easily forgotten in adulthood, we were experiencing a transcending of time and place: of time because the concept of four or five weeks of unadulterated happiness was for us an eternity; of place because Castlecomer was, as my parents often said, a hundred miles away, and thus for a child existed in quite a separate geography. Each year the preparations would follow a pattern. For some days before setting out, my mother washed and ironed, hoping for the sun to pour into the small backyard and garden to dry the lines of garments set out in morning oblation. With tongs she took from the fire the red-hot stones that heated the iron, and the

44

piles of sweet-smelling clothes would grow high on the kitchen table. In the evening before departure my father would come home early from work. His role year after year was to pack the bags. He would achieve the impossible, though not without various mutterings and exasperated expletives. Finally it would be time for us to have our baths before going to bed early, where we would exchange ecstatic plans and hopes before sleep came.

It is the morning of our departure, and we savor the rare experience of taking a taxi. It comes up the hill street from the station, a large ancient American car, its own arrival in Ireland probably the whim of some emigrant who had prospered and sent home this wondrous symbol of his success. To sink back in its huge interior is itself an adventure. We come to the bus station and the bags are pulled out of the cavernous trunk and paced on the sidewalk. My father goes along the line of busses looking for the bus for Clonmel. Eventually we are all aboard, the driver and conductor enviable in their peaked caps, the conductor equipped with his large metal ticket dispenser hanging on a shoulder strap. The engine starts, the bus shudders into life.

Waving to our father, faces pressed against the vibrating window, we are off.

Through the city streets we go, over the many bridges that crisscross the great hidden marsh on which the ancient Norse town was first built. Along by the railway station, then by the river for a few miles, passing Blackrock Castle and turning north through villages that sing in the remembering— Tivoli, Dunkettle, Glanmire, Watergrasshill. Faster and faster the hedges fly by as the bus picks up speed between the villages. Horses and carts, donkeys and smaller carts, the odd cyclist, pull aside into the long green grass at the side of the road to let us pass. From time to time we slow down, not quite stopping at a local shop or pub. The door of the bus noisily swings open, the conductor seizes a heavy roll of newspapers and throws them with unerring aim towards the shop doorway, and off we speed again.

Climbing all the time, we move out of Fermoy, passing the army shooting range at Kilworth, our eyes widening at the odd piece of artillery seen behind the line of trees. Somewhere on a hilltop a white cross stands starkly against the sky, half-hidden in the mist. To a child it is somehow "the" cross, yet I will later come to realize that it is a memorial to more recent agonies vaguely referred to by our parents. They are remembering the flying columns, the ambushes, and the deaths all over north Cork less than twenty years previously as the Irish Republic was being born.

Through Mitchelstown we go before turning east, the tires singing their high-pitched song, the voice of the conductor calling out the names of towns and villages—Ballyporeen, Clogheen, Ardfinnan. The blue distant world of the Knockmealdown Mountains rises away to the south, the rolling hills of Tipperary to the north. Turning under the dark bulk of Cahir Castle, the fifteenth-century fortress of the Butler family, rulers of a great part of this southern province, we finally drive along the banks of the River Suir to Clonmel where lunch awaits, to be followed by the thrill of another bus.

All through the long sunny afternoon we climb the low range of hills that brings us out of Tipperary and into Kilkenny. Somewhere on the road down out of the hills there is a house with mysterious dark blue panes in its windows and a fish pond in the garden. Year by year this house assumes greater significance on this journey. Its unseen inhabitants are clothed with fascinating possibilities. I imagine myself entering the house after skirting the fish pond; I open the front door and enter the parlor amid dark formal furniture. The sun, weakened by the blue panes, is throwing strange patterns of light and dark on the floor. Footsteps are approaching the parlor door. Suddenly, before the stranger enters, I am again back in the bus and the house is disappearing behind the hedgerows.

By now it is early evening. My brother, somewhere between waking and sleeping, leans against me as the bus rattles along the road beside the River Nore. Our youngest brother, only a baby, is fast asleep in my mother's arms. The Cathedral of Saint Canice sends its spire and magnificent Round Tower into the evening sky to welcome us. We move through the outskirts of Kilkenny city, swinging at last into the square under the shadow of the great Norman castle of William the Marshall, the seat of the Dukes of Ormond. There across the square is the smaller country bus that will carry us the last twelve miles to Castlecomer.

Here amid parcels from their day's shopping "in the city" my mother meets familiar faces who say the familiar things of long acquaintance about herself and her boys, remarking how we have grown. As the bus moves out of the town, we, half-blinded by the sun now low across the fields, gaze from the front seat of the bus past the burly shoulders of the driver, looking for well-known scenes, until we turn the last corner and come up the straight stretch of road that becomes Kilkenny Street, its row of shops now closed for the day. There at the corner stands the light carriage known as the trap, the black mare between its shafts, our uncle standing at her head. There are greetings, laughter, a flurry of cases and parcels. We climb up into the seats of the well-sprung trap, and head up the hill out of the town.

Adult conversation is impossible with our endless questions. We ask about the farm, about the animals, about the stream through the fields, on and on until the high graceful wheels of the trap stop in front of the house. Quick greetings are given to grandparents before the mad dash to the stable. The other horse stands in his stall, turning his head as we gingerly but affectionately stroke his haunches, his eyes shining in the darkness. From

49

there to the cow barn, the hay barn, the pigs' house, the apple orchard; on to the wooden gate our uncle has made since last year. We swing it wide, standing on the flagstone outside it that bridges the small stream where we will sail ocean liners made of six-inch slivers of wood. There, sloping up from us, an endless green land stretches away until our eyes encounter the long dark wood that crowns the valley and stands as guardian and boundary to our world.

six

A Love Discerned

At the upper end of the square in Castlecomer a low wall topped by high railings defines the creamery. Towards afternoon the yard is empty, the noise of the machinery has died down, the morning voices have fallen silent. Dust swirls where the feet of horses and donkeys clattered a few hours ago, their dung hardening under the sun in the open area in front of the building.

Bringing the milk to the creamery consumes the precious early morning working hours so it is work for old men or boys. Sometimes it is contracted out to a neighbor. The daily journey to the creamery is my time with my grandfather. We fulfill the crite-

ria for the task, he by fullness of age, I by childhood. To me, far from being a task, it is sheer joy.

To begin the adventure we must start the night
before, because the anticipation of the morning
journey began even before sleep came, as I climbed
the stairs to bed. The great black range has its coal
packed down for the night, its fire glowing through
the bars. The stirabout—meal feed for the hens—
is on for the morning. Almost every night neighbors come visiting—it is called rambling—after the
evening chores. They sit smoking and chatting near
the fire. The door to my grandmother's room is
closed. The oil lamp smokes slightly on the yellow
wall. I am reading *The Egyptian Wanderers: A Tale of
the Fourth Century Persecutions* from the small book-
case at the head of the stairs. It was given to a
grand uncle as a school prize in the late 1880s, and
his name is written on the flyleaf in faded copperplate. Forty years in the future I will stand on the
southern outskirts of Beersheba, flanked by a dingy
gas station and a cheap gift shop, looking south-
wards into the Negev Desert and waiting for the
four camels to emerge from this remembered inner
landscape of childhood.

I am given a candle and told to go to bed. The treads of the stair are creaking and steep. At the turn onto the low and narrow landing, all light from downstairs disappears, and the shadows leap and play as I lift my candle higher. The door at the end on the left leads me to the double bed I share with my grandfather. Later he will come with his candle, undressing quietly and donning his long heavy nightshirt. I feel the pressure on the bed as he kneels for his nightly prayers where I knelt perhaps an hour before.

The night is banished with the sunlight pouring in through the small single-paned window high up in the wall, the crowing of the red-combed strutting cock, and the sound of buckets in the dairy below this end wall of the house. When I wake, my grandfather has already been long up. The cows are milked, the full churns are standing in the cart, the sun glinting off their scrubbed aluminum sides. They are warm to the touch from the milk newly taken from the cows. Sacking covers the bench where my grandfather and I will sit. After my hastily grabbed breakfast, we are given the grocery order for the day and reminded to pick up the mail and the newspaper, a reminder as unnecessary as rubrics in an ancient liturgy.

Crossing the farmyard, the iron-bound wheels crunch and squeal on the gravel. We reach the gate, I turn to wave, the donkey breaks into a canter, his harness jingling. The impetus of this will take us over a hump in the road and we are on our way. The two miles to the town are mostly downhill. Sometimes we join a neighbor, seldom passing, always saluting, perhaps remarking on the surrounding fields, particularly if the crop has been damaged by rain or wind or cattle on the loose. We pass the new government cottages, slate-roofed and stark, clotheslines stretching between them. Around them stand goats, hobbled to prevent them wandering, their pointed beards moving as they chew ceaselessly, their eyes dark and wise, their udders heavy with the tart milk that then only the very poor drank.

We know the names in every house, slated or thatched. Wherever there is a face looking out a window or over a half-door, there is a salutation. My presence in the cart is itself a symbol of the returning season. "Abie's grandson is up from Cork," the voices say as we pass. The season comes when I am old enough to be allowed to take the reins of the donkey, feeling his dogged energy passing along my restraining arms as I swell with pride at this public responsibility.

We are in the town now, bumping over the seldom used rails of the train crossing, swinging left to take our place in the line of carts heading slowly into the creamery. My grandfather gets down from the cart and moves around to chat with neighbors. Rejoicing in the freedom, I preside, reins in hand, over the slow, inevitable progress of the donkey, who moves forward willingly if only because he is nibbling at the straw sticking out the back of the cart in front of us.

Gradually we near the heart of the operation. On a high stone platform the supervisor stands at an accounting desk. Behind him through the open doors can be seen the machinery that receives the fresh milk and in turn disgorges skim milk. The high interior of the building is full of steam and it thunders with the roar and clatter of the machines. To me it is a fearful but totally fascinating place.

The supervisor's coal black hair is streaked by the swirling steam; his black Wellington boots glisten. He appears to me as a kind of demon, standing with unassailable authority over a domain of fire and steel where churns are wrenched open as they crash onto the stone platform, their contents hurled into the vast tank, the quality of the milk measured by magic vials that another white-coated figure dips into the white frothing flood. The arm of the skimmed milk container swings out and the churns in our cart, now empty, are positioned under the wet cloth sock. The whole cart shudders as the white steaming milk falls into the wide hungry mouths of the churns, filling until the bubbles foam above the brims. My grandfather and I replace the covers, my heart pounding with excitement, my thoughts anticipating the next duties of the morning.

The post office is the symbol of a mingled history, the once red British crowns on the boxes painted over with a patriotic green. At this time of day the post office is full. The bare boards echo with the tramp of farm boots. The government notices, printed in English and Gaelic, are yellow in glass cases on the wall. Only we children can read both languages, and even we read haltingly in Gaelic as the newly formed republic teaches us to be the first

Gaelic-speaking generation since the late seventeenth century.

Having picked up the mail, we move from the post office to a tree in the square where we tie the donkey. We walk to the small newsagents shop where my grandfather buys his copy of the *Irish Times,* the paper Protestants read. Among the newspapers there stands on the counter a large jar full of golden pillars—foot-long twisted pieces of barley sugar. As part of the morning ritual, my grandfather asks me if I would like one. Since he is becoming increasingly deaf, he points and winks conspiratorially. We both know that I am to consume the last half-inch before we round the corner to the farmyard gate to face parents concerned about dentists and other city things.

Eventually we turn for home again, heading across the railway tracks, up the hill street, and along the green tree-canopied road. Our progress slows and the haunches of the donkey swell and knot as he begins the pull up the side of the valley. My grandfather gestures for us both to get down and walk for a while. Reaching the level ground we climb up again. Sometimes my grandfather lets the reins hang limply in his hands, the sun rising in the sky and warming his heavy country waistcoat. His head nods. Holding the half-consumed candy bar in my left hand, I take the reins from his sleeping fingers, sitting straight and very proud, assuming full responsibility for everything. Now and then I snatch at the long waving grasses at the side of the narrow road. Sometimes in moments of riotous imagination I pretend that my depleted candy bar is a cigarette from which I deposit imaginary ash to the wind with a brave flourish.

Thus within time, yet in a way that is a time out of time, we round the last bend in the road before the farmyard gate. The donkey breaks into a happy jog, the harness jingles, my grandfather wakes, and we go crunching over the graveled yard where my grandmother waits for him in her chair behind the white lace curtains of her room, reaching in anticipation for her reading glasses, opening them with the white twisted fingers of her pain.

She was forty when there came a stiffness, then pain, then the necessity for a stick. Visits to the doctor brought only two walking sticks and, when necessary, the arms of sons and daughters. One day she left the kitchen and sat in the adjoining room. She was never to walk again in the next thirty years.

During that time she and my grandfather continued their quiet love affair, rich with three daughters, two sons, and the memory of a child, my namesake, who would because of early death remain forever five years old.

Every day there were two particular times when they would enjoy each other's company. In the late morning they would read the paper and comment about the world to each other. Later, when the work in the fields was over, he would again sit with her. When she died, her body was buried in the churchyard, as was the custom of those days. It was also the custom that such things happened without involving the children, so my grandmother's death was a distant and mysterious event, seen with puzzlement only through the tears in my mother's eyes.

The following year, summer having come again to the farm, I went there on holiday. One day we were to visit relatives considered distant in that small island world. We drove through the town and over the bridge, I in the back seat with my grandfather, my uncle and my mother in front. As we drove past the gates of the graveled driveway leading to the churchyard where the summer grass was high and green-gold in the sun, my grandfather, thinking he was unobserved, pressed his face against the window of the car and, with a small hidden motion of his hand, waved.

Somehow I knew what he was doing. Our eyes did not meet. Nothing was said. But I have always been aware that for me it was a moment of gentle but immense growing. Like a traveler who comes suddenly to the edge of a great escarpment and sees a country vast and mysterious and lovely, I came to my first understanding of the majesty and the vulnerability of human love.

seven

A Teller of Tales

During the years of childhood there was a hired man on the farm named John Brennan. With the eye of a small boy I recall him vividly. He wore a red scarf or kerchief around his neck—in this he seemed to me to be part of the romantic world of Long John Silver in Robert Louis Stevenson's *Treasure Island*—a cloth cap, trousers precariously held up by lengths of binder twine, and boots with holes in the soles. John smoked a clay pipe with a metal cap on the bowl. He had a heavy mustache that dripped hot brown tea as his face emerged from a great steaming mug during breaks in the summer haymaking.

Even now I like to linger with John Brennan, whom I loved. I use the word seriously, as a child always uses it. There was one whole day—and you know how long a summer day is in childhood—when I became John Brennan. I announced this fact on rising, refusing all day to answer to my own name as I went about doing the kind of things I imagined were John's duties.

He would often tell me of his far travels in earlier years. To this day I do not know whether he had ever been farther than Dublin, if indeed that far—all of seventy miles. But together we went in my imagination, and for all I know in his, to Afghanistan and Baluchistan. I recall now that these were his favorite settings for past adventures, and since they were probably the most distant parts of the earth imaginable, I am inclined to think that both of us traveled on the wings of imagination rather than of John's memory! However, these remain the golden roads I particularly remember.

In terms of today's precise contracting between people—stated working hours, machines to clock in by, union rules to be observed—the contract between my family and John would be incomprehensible, certainly undefinable. The extraordinary thing was that the sense of mutual obligation was so clearly indissoluble. That did not mean that John was under any coercion to stay, nor was my family under any legal obligation to retain him. The bond was deeper, older, more subtle. Without ever expressing itself in terms of feudal relationship and mutual responsibility, it acted on those ancient precedents. For instance, John was not a model of dependability. Sometimes in the morning he had to be sent for, and in the summertime I would be the one chosen to rouse him. Whenever this happened I would also be presented with a clean white galvanized bucket to bring back water from the well below John's cottage.

I always go to find him with mingled fear and excitement. Swinging my bucket, I set out up the winding earthen road sided by grassy banks that rise to high hedges and hide the surrounding meadows. After about half a mile I turn into the long straight lane that leads to John's place. Over the lane the trees meet, creating on sunny days a leafy pavilion floored with dappled earth and stones. Under the skies of an afternoon thundershower the lane becomes for a child a shadowed gallery leading to wildly imagined terrors.

John's cottage stands in a grove of trees overlooking a deep gully where the well sinks deep into the earth. Knowing that I will have to fill the bucket, I leave it by the broken and rusted gate that groans and rattles on its hinges. The cottage is more a ruin than a dwelling. All over Ireland in those days stood the ruined walls of primitive cottages, their thatched roofs long gone. John had partially roofed this ruin and now lived in the solitary space where the chimney formerly stood. Only once had I glimpsed the interior over the open half-door. John had marked off an area with some stones, and within this area he had placed some straw-filled sacks as a mattress. A small crude table stood under the tiny window. On the wall hung a framed Sacred Heart of Jesus. I never again saw the interior. It remained mysterious and fearful, the grove around it becoming in my mind both the home of a beloved friend and the lair of a fearful giant.

I approach the cottage, rounding the ruined wall that frames the part of it open to the sky. I can see from here that the upper part of the door is closed. Grateful for this, I walk as silently as possible until I can knock on the door, poised for flight if it should suddenly open. There is no sound.

Taking a stone, I bang on the door. This time there is an answering growl rising to an angry questioning shout. I cry out, "John, Grandpa says you're to come over!" Immediately after delivering my message I run around the crumbling wall and make for the gate. Taking the bucket I go down to the well, fill the bucket, and race back along the lane until I reach the open roadway.

In those days I learned things from John that I never forgot. About a mile from the farm there was a crossroads, and once John told me that it and all crossroads were mysterious places. He said that we always had to make a choice at a crossroads, and that every such choice in some way changed the pattern of our life. That is why there was an old legend—said John—that very often both God and the Devil were at crossroads, both waiting. Each tried to ensure that the traveler's choice was made in such a way that eventually, by many roads and many more such choices, they would be brought to heaven or to hell. One had therefore, John admonished me, to be very careful at crossroads. They were good places to make the sign of the cross while deciding on a direction to take.

One evening of summer, when the haymaking was over and John and I sat on the long low stone outside the stable door, he pointed out to me that the earliest stars were beginning to appear. When the archangel Gabriel came to announce to the Blessed Virgin Mary her great vocation of giving birth to the Son of God he waited for her refusal or acceptance. John told me that between the angel's annunciation and Mary's acceptance, all the stars in the sky stood still, so important was that moment in time. Only when the Blessed Virgin accepted her vocation did the stars begin again to circle the galaxies.

I also remember another evening, or perhaps I should say a late afternoon. Everyone—meaning my uncles, my grandfather, John, my brother, and I—were in the last and highest field on the farm, the one nearest to Grant's Wood, the long dark wall of tall coniferous trees that crowned the ridge of the valley and began only a couple of fields from where we were.

My brother and I—we were about ten and six—were always frightened of the wood. The few yards that we could see into it only excited our imaginations about what could be hidden in the dark recesses of the trees. John knew this, and one day he asked us if we would like to go into the wood when the work was finished. Fearfully we said yes.

In those long summer evenings—and summer evenings are so long because of the relatively northern latitudes of Ireland—haymaking would continue to as late an hour as possible. So it was not long before sunset when work ceased and John called us to go with him towards the wood. I can remember him so clearly, even after all these years. His old boots were broken, their toes turned up. His ankles were bare, his baggy trousers tied at the knees with twine, a piece of rope supporting it at the waist. He wore a striped shirt, almost certainly a cast-off from my grandfather, with a piece of colored cloth knotted around his neck, his ancient shiny cap balanced precariously forward on his head as he looked down at us affectionately, his eyes full of amused laughter.

We had to go through some scrubland. As we approached the trees they seemed to grow taller and taller until they loomed above us. We both held John's hands. Into the trees we went, gazing around in wonder, stepping over thorns and small branches. We probably went in no more than fifty yards when we realized that the wood was not nearly as dark as we had thought. When we turned to look out from where we stood—keeping very close to John—the light of the setting sun beckoned to us reassuringly.

I cannot recall how long we remained there among the trees—probably not more than a few minutes. Neither can I recall anything significant that was said. John was not given to speeches. If anything, he was much more given to a laughing remark about things. There in the lengthening shadows of the quiet clearing in the wood we really had no need of words. By the simple act of bringing us in among the trees John had shown his sensitivity to our childhood fear in the simplest and most effective way possible. He had taken us by the hand, led us to the place we feared, and shown us that there was nothing to fear. At one and the same moment he had become guide, mentor, guardian. The wood was never quite as frightening again. We still never returned on our own, but we no longer dreaded it as we had done.

Years later, when I was in my late teens, my uncle had to sell the farm that had been in our family for four generations. John was by then in his late eighties; having worked on the farm since he was a young man, he and my grandfather had grown old together. In the last few years he had been able to do only very light work—and that on a part-time basis. On the day of the auction, someone remarked on John's absence. So my cousin went to look for him, walking the half-mile of winding, narrow road with its long grassy bands and high hedges.

John was lying in the long grass as if asleep. In the way that St. Paul described the death of certain disciples, John had simply "fallen asleep." He had left the cottage to come to the auction, and along the way, with a loving Father above and around him, had realized that spring day was the day for work to end and a great journey to begin.

⚙⚙
eight

The End of Innocence

The arch of the stone bridge across the river is high enough to hide the town square of Castlecomer until you come to the center of the bridge. From there the small river flows south between thick overhanging trees. In the still, dark water there once grew huge lily pads. Quiet ripples among them hinted of unseen creatures. Sometimes a bird cried out, its call echoing in the cavern of the trees.

Beyond the bridge, several houses stood in comparative aloofness. Desirable because of their age and location, their Georgian doors and windows gleaming with black paint, these were the houses of the public figures around whom the life of the community revolved—the doctor, the schoolteacher, the bank manager, the Church of Ireland rector. Each of these houses presented to the world an almost Olympian impassiveness. In my memory no child played before their curtained windows. If the gleaming brass of the doors ever swung open, I never witnessed it. Each house had the high distinction of owning a motor car. In front of the houses the great trees, planted along ago around the square, ensured a further degree of dignity, shade, privacy.

Years late I would realize the hidden realities behind those lace curtains and hydrangeas: an old friend of my grandparents, aging and ill, desperately trying to survive with the aid of alcohol, that most treacherous companion of adversity. A merchant using the same device to ensure a constant camaraderie among his more significant customers while trying to deal with a spouse's chronic depression. A schoolteacher valiantly trying to keep up appearances on a small salary. A rector gradually coming to terms with the realization that his ministry would continue in that quiet place until retirement came, all the while remaining faithful and loving to his people.

Further from the bridge, beyond the quiet houses, the shops began. Among these was the butcher's shop of Maurice Doyle. Some years before this Maurice had gone to America. By then he had returned, and, as with all returning emigrants, was regarded by the town as having a faint air of glamour and mystery. He was an affable roughneck whose romantic image was enhanced by a broken nose, a wide gap-toothed grin, and an incipiently nasal accent mingled with his native brogue, not to mention his allusions to cattle ranching in Texas. All this in a small Irish town where cowboy films had only recently begun to be shown twice a week in the town hall made Maurice a somewhat exotic figure.

One hot July afternoon I was outside the shop, having walked down to the town on an errand for my aunt. The square was almost empty because most people were hard at work in the fields. Maurice emerged and began to chat. I was from the distant city of Cork, so by the magic of his charm we became brothers in urban superiority and worldliness, each of us aware of the town as a tiny world. We spoke of Texas, of cattle drives and guns.

I do not know what made Maurice invite me in to see what was about to take place in the shed behind the shop. We went in, walking over the sawdust-covered floor of the shop. We passed the great beef and pork sides hanging on their gleaming hooks, assorted entrails still attached to the rib cages. Crossing the yard, we came to a half-door that Maurice leaned on, gesturing to me to look in. Inside stood a large heavy bullock. The beast's head was lowered, the eyes regarding us balefully from above a large heavy iron ring that held its nose and was attached to the floor by a chain. Around the chain the floor dipped into a hollow, at the center of which I could see a drain. I still did not realize what was about to happen.

Bidding me to wait, Maurice returned to the shop. In a few moments he returned, grinning broadly and carrying a double-barreled shotgun. In his other hand were two shells. Only then did I realize that suddenly, without warning, I was for the first time in my life to witness a violent death. My heart pounded with a spasm of fear and excitement. Flight and fascination battled inside me.

Maurice rested the great gleaming gun on the half-door, squinting down its barrels. Once he turned to me with wild laughing eyes, and then hunched down for the kill. The bullock's front legs were apart, its wide forehead directly in my gaze. My eyes were riveted on this living creature to whom this sunny afternoon was to bring a sudden death. The horrified waiting was shattered by the thunder of the gun. As if drawn together by this dreadful moment into a common death, Maurice's body also staggered back from the kick of the gun. I was conscious of uncontrollable trembling while before us the beast shuddered, a great hole appearing in the center of its forehead. For a moment it continued to stand, then it toppled with a crash to the floor, its body thrashing in spasm. In the stillness of the town's afternoon, I could hear the trickle of blood as it stained the rusty grating and fell into the darkness.

My mind was crowded with images from pages that were already a familiar landscape from school, Sunday school, and home. The words of Genesis emerged into terrifying reality from the seeming calm and peace of Sunday morning worship. This then was what it meant to be given "dominion over every living creature that moves on the earth." This presumably was Peter on the Joppa rooftop being bidden to "arise, kill, and eat." This was Elijah on Mount Horeb, butchering the bullock to test Yahweh and applying the same knife to the throats of the prophets of Baal. This was Abraham plunging the knife into the pulsating throat of the hastily captured ram, grateful that it was not the blood of Isaac his son drenching the rough wooden altar. This was Jesus on the cross, his blood in the gleaming cup on the altar. This was the Sacred Heart pumping the lifeblood of the world above the little lamp on the walls of cottages and small row houses all around me.

My eyes turned from the blood-stained grating. Maurice's excitement had subsided. Saying that he now had work to do, he dismissed me, not unfriendly so much as preoccupied, almost distracted.

I came out into the sunlight of the square and started up the hill out of the town, my small bag of groceries in my hand. My most shattering discovery was the nearness of the killing ground. Until today it had been infinitely distant. That animals were killed I had realized: I had frequently known of the frantic deaths of farmyard hens. My uncle would enter the henhouse. In the unseen darkness there would be sudden sounds, the scrambling of claws, the beating of wings. He would emerge with the chosen bird, keeping the knife hidden from me as he passed.

Today had been a greater and more thunderous reality. Images of death seemed to be on every side of me, where before there had only been things of the day taken for granted. In my imagination I looked through Maurice's eyes down the long gleaming barrel and saw a human face rather than that of a beast. The small hospital that I could see from a certain bend in the road became a dreaded place even in the summer sunlight. I thought with terror of the side chapel in the Church of the Immaculate Conception where I had sometimes seen a gleaming coffin flanked by flowers and candles, awaiting its time for requiem mass.

All the way home I was aware that things would never be the same again. I recalled the terrible high squealing of pigs that had often punctuated sunlit days, carried on the breeze across meadows to me as I played with my brothers. I realize I had been sheltered in innocence by a benign adult conspiracy that was only too familiar with the sights and sounds of death. From now on no such shelter would be available. I had been taken beyond the first frontier of a mysterious country that lies beyond childhood lands. From now on sunlight and shadow would always mingle in my experience. I had encountered death. We had met in such a place and in such a way that my childhood became partner to what is perhaps death's most terrible secret: as with the mystery of birth, death walks in the most normal and ordinary of places. The sacred child comes to birth in the rude manger, the sacred bull comes to the slaughter in a country shed.

A Pastoral World

It was significant in those days that church and chapel were at opposite ends of the town. The Roman Catholic church, never called anything other than "the chapel" by Church of Ireland people, was by far the larger. For me the bell of Saint Mary's pealed gently, while that of the Church of the Immaculate Conception boomed authoritatively! I loved the one and, I confess, feared the other.

Immaculate Conception had the eternal fascination of the totally forbidden. No Islamic prohibition on the outskirts of today's Mecca has more absolute authority than that prohibition had in our lives. As if both to warn and to tantalize, like the shimmering mirage in the desert that draws an unwary traveler from the right path, the blaze of what I now know to be the votive candle stand could be seen deep within the shadowed interior as one stood outside the huge doors. Many years later I would look at the tray of votive candles in my own parish church, placed as a simple and lovely pastoral aid for those who wished to offer an intercession for others, and I would see again the tiny brilliant flames flickering in the shadows of Immaculate Conception.

On Sundays along the narrow country roads, neighbors would answer the bells that called them respectively to mass or matins, benediction or evening prayer. In Donaguile the pony would be harnessed to the shafts of the trap. Cows newly milked would long since be back in the fields. Families saluted one another as they met, sometimes pulling to the side of the road to allow others to pass as they returned home from an earlier service. In one high trap drawn by a huge horse, I recall a boy about my own age who had what I now know to be Down's Syndrome. My memory is that he was severely affected. Even though hidden in the shelter of a large farm during the week, he would be dressed to join the family for mass. To me it was an indication of the power of the mass that this other boy, who both fascinated and alarmed me, probably because in age and coloring we were alike, was brought fully into the community for that strange mysterious rite carried out beyond my vision and chanted in an ancient tongue.

The presence of the priest, the nun, and the friar was so common in that long ago Ireland that I can think of no parallel other than the legions of saffron-robed monks in the streets of a Burmese city. They were absolutely woven into the town's life. They shared a railway carriage or a bus. They passed by us on the street. At a school sports meeting they were often the umpires, the sleeves of their habits rolled up on a sunny day, their fingers browned by nicotine, their beards beaded with strong brown tea. The one consistent thing was that they were almost never seen alone, but appeared in pairs or groups. This had the effect of their both mingling in society yet being a step apart from it.

So it was that I became aware of two modes of spiritual authority in my childhood, one experienced directly, the other only by hearsay and observation. There seemed to be two modes by which the things of God were mediated and communicated in the community, both hierarchical and both in their own way authoritative. In both churches in town the senior figure was called the canon. Both obviously held positions of great significance in their respective congregations. I suspect that because of the large difference in numbers there could not be the degree of intimacy between clergy and people at Immaculate Conception as there was at Saint Mary's. The former had a large staff of priests, while at Saint Mary's there was the canon and the curate. The canon was permanent, the curate transitory. To be visited by the curate was a pleasant diversion; to be visited by the canon was a serious occasion.

In my childhood the canon was a shy and rather austere man, which made him seem remote in manner. But such was the immense trust between clergy and people in Ireland that no mannerism or quirk of personality could ever break it. Small-talker or not, reserved or hearty, the canon would always be given a warm welcome. He in his turn, in spite of the rigidly graded social universe of the Irish countryside, would have been hurt and dismayed if anyone had imputed that even the humblest home had not received his utmost pastoral attention and care in a time of need.

I remember an afternoon in late summer on the farm shortly before we returned to the city and to school. My grandmother, seated in her window chair, suddenly cried, "The canon is coming!" My aunt flew to the half-door. Coming up the driveway was indeed the canon. He was pedaling slowly, his eyes towards the ground, doubtless pretending not to notice the feverish activity he was well aware would be precipitated by his approach. The hill up from the town had taken its toll. I suspect that his thoughts were on such things as a strong cup of tea.

In swift succession my aunt cast her apron in a corner, tidied her hair, put a kettle on the range, paused to collect herself, and went out to greet the visitor. The kitchen darkened as they filled the doorway. The canon entered, tall and imposing. There were greetings, and my hand was shaken from a great height. My grandmother was greeted. Only then was the key taken down from over the parlor door. This was in itself a measure of the significance of this moment. The parlor was a forbidden land, attainable only on special occasions. It contained a large table, a black leather couch, some chairs, a large sideboard with a mirror, photographs—some yellowing—of various family members and occasions of gathering. All this with some old copies of the *Daily Sketch* for the year 1936, when England had had three kings—George V, Edward VIII, and George VI. As a special privilege I was sometimes allowed to look at the solemn events on these pages.

The canon and my aunt went to the parlor. My grandmother's chair was pushed on its small wheels down into the room, and I was sent to find my mother, who was feeding my baby brother. Then I was to go to the hayfield and inform my grandfather and uncles that the canon was in the house. I was unaware that this was all an age-old and well-rehearsed liturgy wherein all the players knew their parts. The canon knew that the men would be called in; he therefore came near the end of the working afternoon so that they would not lose more than the minimum of sunlit hours in the fields. The men knew that they had some leeway while tea was prepared for the canon. This was a universe of tradition and predictability.

When I returned, my mother and my two brothers were in the parlor. My aunt was preparing tea—hot apple pie and fresh griddle bread with salty farm butter and jam. As if all was being coordinated by an unseen director, tea was ready and laid on the table just as my grandfather and uncles arrived from the fields. They had thrown water on their faces and hands from the rain barrel. Greetings were exchanged, comments on the weather and the crops made, and heads were bowed while the canon said the grace over the food. He prayed for the family, speaking loudly enough so that my grandfather could hear. My baby brother cried and was hushed. I suddenly remembered a simple lullaby I was then learning in school. The lines were written by an Irish poet, Padraic Culum.

O men from the fields!
Come softly within,
Tread softly, softly,
O men coming in.
Mavourneen is going
From me and from you,
Where Mary will fold him
With mantle of blue.

It was a moment for life-long remembrance: a gathered family, the layers of generations, the sun-lit fields, the richness of simple food, the church embodied in the tall figure at the table. For a child earth and heaven were for a moment one.

∞
ten

The Family
of God

In the 1930s the life of a child of the Church of
Ireland was centered in the life of that church.
Almost every Church of Ireland family in those
days was churchgoing and would have been known
personally to the rector of the parish. We ourselves
lived almost literally in the shadow of the church,
our house down a narrow hill street about a hundred and fifty yards from the church door. I now
realize that the church was far more than an institution in those days. At no time did we think or
speak of it as such. It was much more a character in
the small drama of our lives. It played many
parts—friend, counselor, teacher, storyteller, source

of our identity, provider of community. Looking back, it would be difficult for me to name an aspect of life in which the church did not in some way touch my life.

The parish school, a large two-roomed building, was subsidized by both church and government, an agreement made when the new republic was born in 1923, only five years before my own coming into the world. The school was regularly visited by the rector. The establishment where our teachers were trained was called the Church of Ireland Training College, and at least once a year the parish school would on separate occasions be inspected by a government inspector and the diocesan examiner, the latter a priest of the diocese.

It was to this diocese that my mother and father, struggling to survive in the depression years of the thirties, applied for a scholarship for their two boys of school age. I recall very clearly the day when the rector sat in the parlor of our home and made the suggestion that we might apply for a scholarship for my continued schooling, my mother leaning forward eagerly, my baby brother in her arms, while I stood diffidently against the arm of the sofa. From there things rapidly moved to obtaining my father's approval, which was eagerly and readily given. His copperplate handwriting—of which he was very proud—filled out the application, which I duly took to the rectory, running up the street, turning into the gravelled driveway to push the large mother-of-pearl bell by the black Georgian door.

In the fullness of time the rector came again to our house. My application had been received and I was to present myself at a meeting of the diocesan committee on a certain date. The morning of the great day was noteworthy if only for the fact that I had been given permission to be absent from school for part of the day. The night before my best suit was laid out—my best and only suit, usually referred to as my Sunday suit. A bath was insisted upon. Whatever the outcome of the day, I would go before my benefactors sweet smelling and shining!

Thus we set out for the long walk to the diocesan offices, my mother suitably attired for a most important occasion, my youngest brother in his pram, myself spotlessly clean, hair brushed, shoes polished, socks gartered so that they would not crumple about my ankles.

The diocesan offices were imposing, fronted by steps that called for great effort with our pram.

Dark paneling sobered the visitor. High-ceilinged halls and stairs spoke of places of vast and varied importance. In the dim hallway we could see two other families gathered for what I assumed to be the same purpose as ours.

We waited outside a large door on either side of which frosted glass hid the activity within. When our name was called we were invited in and asked to sit. We were at one end of a large gleaming boardroom table, at the other end of which sat the bishop, flanked by the dean and an archdeacon. Beyond these three the mists have closed in to hide the faces of what were almost certainly sundry prominent diocesan laity. Perhaps it needs to be said that in those days such ecclesiastical dignitaries were so far above us in the accepted scale of things that it was rather like being a suppliant before the throne of Zeus flanked by a brace of lesser deities.

The questioning was kindly, aimed at putting my mother at ease. I am quite sure that in the world of that church family the scholarship was ours even before entering. At one stage the dean, a pleasant florid man with a mane of white hair, pushed himself back from the table, crossed his gaitered legs and asked my mother if I was the only

child. When she said that there were two other
boys the dean expressed a chortling pleasure at this
major contribution to the dwindling population of
the Church of Ireland. "Well done, Mrs.
O'Driscoll," he exclaimed, "well done indeed, with
your three fine boys in the church." We departed
with the assurance that our application would be
given every consideration. Within a week or two a
large envelope arrived at the house informing my
parents that I was the recipient of a princely two
pounds and ten shillings a quarter year. That shining fifty shillings came regularly until I departed
the parish school and prepared for what was then
called secondary school. Here again the church
would be prepared to take care of her own.

Now it is my twelfth birthday and my last year
in parish school. Our father is seriously ill. He lies
upstairs and we are to be as still as energetic boys
are capable of being. The doctor comes, a gentle
and caring woman who is also the bishop's wife. I
watch her go upstairs and return again to speak to
my mother in the garden. I watch from the window, knowing that I am not meant to overhear this
conversation that is so far from casual. From that
day my memories of my father are of constant

exhaustion, weekends of resting, and an increasingly limited ability to share in our changing lives. Some years later my mother spoke of that day. "Doctor Mary said to me that she thought she could patch your father up for about ten years until you boys were grown." The good doctor's skill and care did exactly that, almost to the day: my father died the summer before I began my last year in theology.

It was no accident in the close church network of our little world that the headmaster of a nearby Church of Ireland boarding school arrived at our door within weeks of Doctor Mary's visit. He spoke of the possibility of another scholarship that would allow me to go to Midleton College, a boarding school for boys. I would sit for an examination for a scholarship. At intervals in the following years both my brothers would be recipients of the same scholarship and would themselves become boarders.

All during that last term of parish schooling I stayed late for extra tutoring. Mr. Coulter, the principal of the parish school, could not have been more generous with his time. Every day after school he would personally tutor the two of us who were to be presented for scholarships. A measure of his anxiety about the outcome was the bamboo cane that rested on the small desk in front of him, a cane that was used from time to time on our lower legs, especially as time drew near for the examination.

The great day came when I was deposited at the railway station clothed in my best—and only—suit, with two pens (the school would supply paper and ink for the examination) and a clean handkerchief. My mother was adamant about the clean handkerchief. There followed some anxious weeks of waiting, until the envelope duly arrived from the school, congratulating me on having done an excellent examination and informing me that I would begin as a boarder on September 9, 1941.

With the letter comes a list of things I will need for my life in school. The list is strongly trinitarian. Three of almost everything: three pairs of socks, three shirts, three sets of underwear, three sets of pyjamas. One coat, one pair of gloves, one school cap, one Bible, one *Book of Common Prayer,* one pair of rugby boots, one hockey stick. I will wear my clothes for a week, at the end of which I will be given a change. A spare set of everything will remain in the linen room of the school.

Thus I would live for four years in a regimen whose motto to this day is *Spatian Nactus Es, Hanc Exorna:* "You are a Spartan; live up to it." In those four years I would walk to the village church in a line of twos once every Sunday and twice on the last Sunday in the month for evening prayer. Once a year a missionary would arrive complete with magic lantern slides of far-flung parts of the empire. I had a missionary box into which I was bidden to place my precious pennies for work in such places as western Canada—where, in the irony of life, I now sit as I write. I would attend confirmation classes in the study of the local rector's house, relishing at least a glimpse of the comforts of home as a relief from the rigors of school. I would have scripture classes each week. Once each year at the approach of what was referred to as "the Synod"—an examination set by the church for all ages—the school would stop all other subjects and for about two weeks we would do nothing else from nine to three other than Old Testament, New Testament, and church doctrine. Eventually I would sit in the diocesan cathedral with some scores of other boys and girls prepared for confirmation, listening with varying degrees of concentration to

the bishop's two homilies—one before our confirmation and one afterwards—each twenty-five minutes long.

The bishop is a large and nervous man, his dic-
tion rather plaintive and breathless. He folds his
hands so that the ruffles of his episcopal cuffs form
a great white blossom constantly being shaken as if
in a wind. His head tends to be slanted to one side.
From time to time he places his hands to his cheek
as if preparing to sleep, then suddenly sweeps them
apart as he pleads with us to become mindful of
some particular truth about the Christian life, a life
he constantly refers to as a battle, enunciating the
word so decisively that he invariably stutters, much
to our delight.

And so the way stretched ahead and my journey
to the priesthood continued. I would come to call
other parts of the larger church home. I would
come to realize that the gaitered giants of my childhood were no more fearsome than the wizard of Oz.
I would see the church diminished and in many
ways humbled. I would come to realize in myself
that priesthood does not confer the overcoming of
one's humanity, yet that Christian faith and fellowship can do much to sustain one in the struggle.

Above all, I would never cease to be grateful to the church for the guidance given me and the love shown to me in its fellowship.

eleven

Glendalough

It is late September 1999 and a light mist is gathering over the upper lake in Glendalough. The small hotel nestles at the end of the lower lake and from it there is a choice of walks. For some reason this area, even though it is in the Wicklow Mountains and within easy driving distance of Dublin, has not yet been spoiled. During the weekends there is an influx from the city but for the rest of the week there is a quiet friendly atmosphere, the guests in the hotel sparse enough to smile warmly and to remark on this or that as they pass one another on the patterned carpets by wooden paneling smoothed by time. The one area that remains splendidly noisy and filled is the lounge bar, where locals and visitors mingle from lunch time to late evening over tea and scones, beer, wine, whisky, sandwiches, and a good selection of pub fare.

In Gaelic, Glendalough means "the valley of the two lakes." The hills around the valley are steep and high and wooded. For about thirteen hundred years this valley has been a place of Christian pilgrimage since Kevin, a sixth-century monk, came over the pass from County Kildare and found himself beside these two small lakes. On the high ground beside the lower lake he built his hut, as was the custom of those days, and gradually around him there gathered others who came because they wished to be in the company of a holy man. Sometimes they left again, wandering on out of this valley in search of other such places. Sometimes they stayed to join the community in its life of manual labor, farming, and worship.

Many more stayed than left, until here in the valley stood what became known as a monastic city, its surrounding wall protecting it, its huts for individuals and families dotted around, and in the center the place of worship. With time the fragile huts would eventually become stone, and beside them a high round tower would soar, protection against the marauding Norsemen of the eighth and ninth centuries.

Kevin would find, as many holy men and woman after him, that sanctity mingled with fame has its price. In an effort to claim his life as his own he moved away from the circle of the monastery, searched the upper lake for a suitable dwelling place, and selected a cave high up in the cliff overlooking the water. This became known as his desert, the place where he could commune and pray as he wished. Tradition has it that he never returned, though many would seek him out, walking the upper reaches of the valley that skirt along the shoreline of the lakes.

Even today, in this age of inevitable change, little has changed here. The hotel is almost half of the little village. The education center for visitors does not intrude. Tucked behind the hotel overlooking the Glendassan River, the center is tasteful and modest, having to this point escaped the ministrations of public relations experts and their determined promoting. In a word, Glendalough has not yet become a product.

My destination is not towards the lakes but eastward along the southern slope of the valley. I have already taken this walk with others and now I want to take it by myself, wishing to return to a place that draws me back to it. I set out through the parking lot, cross the small bridge, and head across the flat floor of the valley to where the river is joined by the waters coming from the lower lake. Here is another small bridge up to the earthen surface of the Green Road, where I turn eastward. On my right is the gradual slope of the Derrybawn (White Oaks) Mountain, on my left the fall away of the valley towards the river I have just crossed over.

For the most part the road continues under a roof of trees. I am walking through a wood that barely allows the narrow road to run through its precincts. On my left I pass an ancient spot called Saint Kevin's Well, now heavily overgrown and almost lost in the undergrowth, but I have another destination in mind.

After about twenty minutes I turn off the road, climb over a low stone wall, and move down among the trees. The descent is gradual and I have to be mindful of tree roots. The light changes as I descend among the trees until once again I am on the floor of the valley. It is silent here, no breeze stirring. To each side of me the avenues of trees stretch away into the dim light. I pass out of the trees towards a low wall, high enough to need rough steps up to its grassy top, and there within its stone enclosure is Saint Savior's Church. Just beyond it is the Glendassan River once again, the low murmur of its flow filling this open area.

Saint Savior's was built here six hundred years after Kevin began his monastic city. There is a certain sadness to the story of why it was built. By this time the quality of Irish monastic life was flagging, and a reforming abbot named Laurence O'Toole decided to bring in one of the new monastic orders flourishing in England and the continent. In this case it was the Augustinian Canons who came here from Canterbury. Laurence's hope was that these highly disciplined monks with their vision of a renewed and sterner monastic life would in turn renew the life of a Glendalough wearied—as Laurence viewed it—by age and isolation. I can still see the stone steps that climb to what was once their living quarters beside the church.

Today Saint Savior's is a ruin. For me it is a place of particular beauty and peace, although I am not sure why it draws me as it does. There is the stillness, made all the more remarkable by the voice of the nearby river. There is the presence of time, untold millennia in the surrounding nature, at least eight hundred years in these walls that now hold little more than rain pools and tufts of grass. Saint Savior's is a good place to do that most difficult of things, to be alone with oneself and to be at peace.

I have deliberately not brought something to read—my constant temptation at such times—but simply sit on the stone bench that juts out from part of the wall. There has been rain earlier in the day but for now the sky looks reasonably benevolent. My early years in Ireland have taught me to ask for no guarantees from the weather gods!

I find myself thinking of many things, letting my thoughts flow freely. I think of the gift of this short time in this valley, the pleasant company of the group among whom I travel. I think of our children and grandchildren back in Canada. The fact that in a few weeks I shall be seventy years old steals into the silence. Perhaps as a natural detour from this I think of growing up in this country, attending university not fifty miles from here, yet rarely then becoming aware of the long heritage of Christian faith all around me. Perhaps the present rather than the past is the natural habitat of the young.

Intellectually I had always known something of the story of Irish Celtic Christianity. An essay by John Henry Newman, read in the senior grades of boarding school, had excited me about "The Isles of the North," as Newman called them, in the fifth to the seventh centuries. I had always known the giants of the story—Patrick, Bridget, Columba, Kevin—but it was not until I left Ireland that they and their time began to excite me. It was not that I dismissed them in any way, merely that I took them for granted in the long story of the church into which I had been born. I think it is a fairly universal experience that if you live in a place that surrounds you with many layers of the past, you tend to take them for granted. Sometimes when somebody comes from a younger world and is fascinated by what you yourself have taken for granted, you feel a twinge of guilt for your neglect along with pleasure at their excitement.

But something extraordinary has happened since I left Ireland in 1954. For reasons that no one quite understands but many guess at, the story of Christian faith in Ireland, and in the islands small and large that lie to its east and north, has begun to impinge on the faith journeying of millions of people for whom the word Celtic has come to hold a remarkable fascination. The community life of this lovely Glendalough area, rich and varied long before the mushrooming life of nearby Dublin had even begun, excites and intrigues Christians today in a way that the earnest reforming work of the later orders—Lawrence O'Toole's Augustinian Canons and the Cistercians—has not. I find myself wondering why. I glance over at the archway that once held the door to the refectory where these twelfth-century reformers ate their meals. I can so easily imagine their contemptuous dismissal of the Irish church foundations further up the valley.

Yet they are largely forgotten, while the memory of Kevin shines on and beckons to Christians today. I find myself asking what it was about the simplicities—even the crudities—of these sixth-century Christians that speaks so eloquently at this particular time in history. Why does it speak more than anywhere else to those of us living today in North America? Why is it that if I were offered the choice of meeting one of the two people who were spiritual giants in this place—Kevin in the sixth century and Lawrence in the twelfth—I would unhesitatingly choose the former, as would most of my Christian contemporaries who come to this valley?

I cannot help thinking that such a choice is in some way linked with the perception we have, real or imagined, that a certain simplicity of Christian faith and community ended with the passing of the Celtic way. I deliberately use the word "way" rather than "church" because it is quite wrong to think of Christians such as Kevin here in Glendalough, Columba on Iona, and Bridget in Kildare as in any way perceiving themselves as of a church other than the One Holy Catholic Church. They might resent it at times, criticize it, rail against its interference, or write strong letters of protest, but they would always have seen themselves as of it and within it. Perhaps, if nothing else, this may speak as a corrective to the readiness of some in today's church to form splinter movements.

Between the time that Kevin first walked over the pass into this valley and Lawrence came to guide the community six centuries later, much had happened in the great outside world. It was necessary to find sterner and more resilient ways to form Christian faith and community. Beliefs that had been held with simple joy and passion were transformed into a system of intellect and sophistication. I who sit here today in Saint Savior's, as far in Laurence's future as Kevin was in his past, am of a church and time that is weary and mistrustful of intellect and sophistication in matters of faith, longing again for simplicity and passion.

The clouds are coming in over the valley from the west and I must leave. I stand for a moment in the middle of the ruined church, estimating where the center aisle might once have been. I stand facing the ruins of the sanctuary. I try to imagine being among the canons as they celebrated mass, full of good intentions for the edification and improving of their dreamy, lazy Irish brethren, not to mention their brazen women who had scant respect for foreign cowls and accents. So confident these canons must have been that they embodied the future, little suspecting that it was those whom they dismissed who would speak to a faraway generation hungrier for things of the spirit and the imagination than for things of the intellect. As I climbed the wall and entered the trees the first drops of the shower began to fall.

❦
twelve

Turning Back

I began these meditations by turning away from Donaguile, feeling a sense of pleasure that I had been able to break the cord that allowed it such a huge place in my life. Yet I know that the cord is merely loosened, not broken, and that I will come again into the town square and this time will not turn away. I will find some excuse to go up the road, noting the many changes but restoring in my mind's eye what was once there: the police barracks with its high walls pockmarked from the troubles of the 1920s, the house with its small coal business that made it and everything around it black, the quarry with its still water reflecting clouds by day and stars by night. Passing the quarry, I know, will bring a surge of anticipation, the turning of the last corners, the straight stretch beside the cornfield, then the gates, and, about a hundred yards in, the house.

As always in returning to places remembered from childhood, I will marvel again at the change of scale. The two storeys are much lower than I remember. There is a new wing built on, but the farm buildings are much the same. I know that I will not go through the gates, though on one of his visits my brother did go in and the family who now live there were warm in their welcome. My own encounter with the family came in a very different way. I had written of the farm some years ago and the pages managed to find their way to the rectory of a large Roman Catholic parish in New York. There someone realized that it was his father who had bought the farm in Donaguile from my uncle in the 1950s. He wrote me a letter saying that he was eight years old when the family moved onto the farm. Because he and I were about the same age he had memories of the farm very like mine, and these memories had stayed with him into his adult years, as they have with me. The cast of the play had changed for him. He never knew John Brennan, since John had died on the day the farm was sold. But he had known other figures of my childhood who died as they had lived, in utter simplicity, innocent of any world beyond Donaguile itself and the neighboring town.

The town of Castlecomer retains much the same appearance as in my childhood. In the square the donkey carts and the horse traps have been replaced by the same rows of gleaming automobiles that have covered every village and town in Ireland. The cluster of Georgian houses at the end of the square by the bridge are well kept, the brass on the doors shining, the fanlights dusted and clean. The creamery, built in a late Georgian style, is no longer in use. Its yard is quiet, the morning noise and clatter of gleaming machinery and milk cans that was once so frightening to me was silenced some time after the Second World War.

Anyone returning to look at remembered places, especially places of childhood memory, comes to realize that which side of the Atlantic you come from makes a real difference. In North America, returning to childhood places usually means coming to terms with physical change. Very often the farm has become a subdivision, the old school a multilevel parking building. Obviously this is not always true, but it happens much more frequently than in Ireland and the rest of Europe. There one can be lulled into thinking that little has changed because, apart from the number of automobiles, most villages and small towns in Ireland are easily recognized by anyone returning after forty or even fifty years. The small houses, the muted colors of the buildings, the narrow streets, the aging statues, the ubiquitous pubs, the tiny shops, all look the same as memory wishes them to be.

But even a short visit alerts the returning traveler to the fact that behind this facade everything is different. From the small houses sons and daughters leap into cars to gather in pubs, night clubs, and coffee bars in old Georgian houses outside town. Older folk, in whose youth a trip to Dublin was an occasion for wonder, now crowd the airports for the delights of southern Spain or the Madeiras, all expenses included in the bargain price. The small newsagent's shop that I remember never carried anything more exotic than the Dublin papers, a few magazines, English comic books, and *Our Boys,* an earnest and patriotic weekly designed to win my generation away from the lure of English comics.

Now it is flooded with newspapers and magazines from all over Europe and North America.

I order coffee in a small shop. It is still recognizable as the place where I came with my aunt one long ago summer afternoon. I realize now that, good and generous soul that she was, my aunt was as excited as I. Word had gone out that it would soon be possible to purchase in this very shop a "glass ice cream." This meant a scoop of ice cream served in a glass dish with a little fruit-flavored cordial to make it even more desirable. I assume that some enterprising soul in those faraway 1930s had heard of the delights of the soda fountain in America and had decided to produce a modest version of these temptations in his own hometown.

Even today, when my capacity for ice cream sundaes is of necessity more disciplined, I never indulge in one of the bloated descendants of that first modest ice cream in a glass without recalling its arrival on the table in front of me: the unfamiliarity of the long slim spoon, the dipping deep into the luscious depths, the ecstasy of the first mouthful. I remember that my aunt chose lemon cordial while I chose raspberry. Having scraped up the very last signs of the ice cream, we lifted our heavy grocery bags, paid for our indulgence, returned to the pony and trap tethered to one of the trees in the town square, and began the slow journey up Barrack Street and back to the farm.

I long to search for such memories, to find them, to savor them, to discover somewhere in the fields and roads of Donaguile a remembered moment that will allow me to be a child in them just a little longer. I like to think—perhaps everyone does—that my motive arises out of gratitude rather than nostalgia. I learned in these fields and winding country roads that the world has much beauty in it, that among its people are those who love me and whom I love. I learned to play and to perpetrate my share of mischief with younger brothers and cousins. I learned from my grandfather that even adults kneel down beside the bed to say their prayers before sleeping, and from him and my grandmother I learned that married love can share great burdens yet grow richer and deeper with time. I learned that my father, who for the rest of the year was busy and distracted by a workplace of great stress that he cordially loathed, could spend time with us, laughing loudly, hitting a ball a vast distance, repairing a radio, helping to bring in the hay, and in general becoming in the two short weeks of his holiday a very different person to us who loved him.

I realize that for me Donaguile was a world without pain or death, or, should I say, that is how it appeared then. To a child much remained unseen and unheard; much, I realize now, was carefully hidden. Sometimes pain and illness, death and sorrow would come along the quiet roads and would be spoken of in hushed voices, muted even more in the presence of a child. My grandmother had been struck down in her forties by rheumatoid arthritis, but because I had never been aware of her other than being seated in her chair, I perceived this state as normal for her. I can recall being dimly aware of the great sorrow in a neighboring family when one of its members was leaving for Australia, a place so distant in those days that it was assumed there would be no return, at least not for a very long time. I think I gradually picked up the fear of the old hospital building left over from British army days on the outskirts of town, a place always linked more with dying than with recovery. But, apart from these things, the instinctive immortality of childhood made possible a world of largely unalloyed joy.

Recently I have become aware of a Japanese saying: "Until the age of seven a child lives with the gods." With great gratitude I know it was true for me even beyond that age. I find myself wondering whether the reason I am unable to let go of Donaguile is that in those early years I was given what *The Book of Common Prayer* calls "an inestimable benefit," one that moves me to say of those remembered fields and roads and buildings what Jacob exclaims as he wakes from his dream of angels: "This is none other than the house of God, and this is the gate of heaven."